This book belongs to:

I'm No Different Than You

Written by Jaime Mahaffey & Kristy High

Illustrated by DG

Dedication

This book is dedicated to our Lord and Savior, Jesus Christ, who is the head of our lives, and to our families and friends who have always been supportive of our dreams.

We also dedicate this book to all the sickle cell disease super heroes of the world. We will continue to pray for a cure.

ACKNOWLEDGMENTS

Kayla and Kiera, you are our inspiration. Your strength and perseverance knows no bounds. It is an honor to know your story and a privilege to love you.

Izon, may you rest in peace. Your mark on this world will never be forgotten and will continue to live on through this book.

Hi, my name is Kayla. I'm 10 years old and I'm a typical girl. I like unicorns, writing, and listening to music. I'm in the 5th grade and will be going to a new school soon to start 6th grade.

I'm nervous about starting a new school because I don't know how the kids will react when they find out I have sickle cell disease. I had a special test done on my blood when I was born and that's how my parents discovered I have sickle cell disease. When I got older, they started teaching me about sickle cell disease and how to take care of myself.

My doctor explained that sickle cell disease is a genetic condition I was born with. It causes my red blood cells to look different. Instead of being soft and round like a donut, a lot of my red blood cells are shaped like a sickle and are hard and sticky. This makes it difficult for them to move through my body and sometimes they get stuck. When that happens, it causes pain due to limited blood and oxygen flow to parts of my body. My doctor calls it a pain crisis. I need to go to the hospital, get medicine to make me feel better, and make sure I don't have any other medical complications.

My mom always says it takes a special superhero like me to battle sickle cell disease. Friends at my old school knew how to help me when I wasn't feeling well, but they won't be with me at my new school.

"Good morning boys and girls. We have a new student joining us today," my teacher announced. "Now let's all make Kayla feel welcomed."

Everyone had been nice to me so far. Amy and her mom even brought my homework to me when I missed school last week. My mom explained to Amy's mom that I was in the hospital because of a pain crisis.

When I went back to school, all the kids treated me differently. They didn't want to play with me at recess or sit next to me during lunch. I was so confused, sad, and angry. I thought Amy, Chloe, and Cecelia were my friends and I didn't understand why they were being so mean! I just wanted them to like me and be my friends. The next day, I decided to sit next to Amy, Chloe, and Cecelia like I used to.

"What do you think you're doing?" Chloe asked as I sat down with my lunch tray. "I'm eating lunch with you all... my friends!" I told them. "We don't want you near us," Cecelia quickly replied. "Yeah, ewww- go away!" Chloe said as she turned her back toward me. With tears swelling in my eyes, I thought, *how could my friends treat me this way?* Amy said, "I'm sorry Kayla, but we don't want to catch sickle cell disease from you."

When I got home from school, I just laid in my bed and cried. I couldn't understand why Chloe, Amy, and Cecelia thought they could catch sickle cell disease from me. "What's wrong Kayla?" Mom asked. "Did you have a bad day at school?" I didn't want Mom to worry or be burdened with another one of my problems. Mom hugged me and said "Everything will be alright. Whatever is going on, I will help you."

I couldn't hold back my tears any longer. I collapsed into her arms as I cried. "Chloe, Amy, and Cecelia don't want to be around me. They think I will give them sickle cell disease. I thought they were my friends. I'm never going back to school. I just can't face them again Mom!" "I'm sorry that happened to you," Mom said as she wiped away my tears.

"Sometimes people are afraid of things they don't understand. Maybe Chloe, Amy, and Cecelia don't know what sickle cell disease is. Maybe, if you explained it to them, they would no longer be afraid."

My mom spent the rest of the night giving me ideas and ways I could talk to the other kids about my sickle cell disease. I spent the next few weeks coming up with a master plan of what I was going to say, not only to Chloe, Amy, and Cecelia, but to all the people in my school. I was determined to help them understand that, even though I have sickle cell disease, I am no different than them.

As I sat in class, I decided today would be the day. I was going to teach them everything I knew about sickle cell disease and let them know they didn't have to be afraid of me. Suddenly, the teacher announced, "Class, we have a special presentation today." In walks someone from my doctor's office. It's Mr. Whitehurst! He works at my doctor's office and helps kids and families teach others about sickle cell disease. He must be here to help me explain sickle cell disease to everyone. This is what my mom meant when she said she would help me.

Everyone listened carefully as Mr. Whitehurst spoke. "Why can't you just take medicine to make sickle cell disease go away forever... you know, like a cure?" Samuel asked. "Well, for right now, there is no cure for sickle cell disease. But researchers are looking for one." Chloe raised her hand and asked, "Can someone with sickle cell disease give it to you if they touch you or sneeze on you?" "Sickle cell disease is not contagious, boys and girls." Mr. Whitehurst explained. "You can't catch it from someone. It is passed down through genes you get from your mom and dad, just like brown eyes or dimples. It's the way you are born, and no one should be treated differently because of the way they are born."

Mr. Whitehurst went on to explain, "Kids with sickle cell disease are just like every other kid. They want to play with their friends and they want other people to understand that, while they do have some special health needs, they can do anything you can. It is very important to include them in activities and treat them with kindness and understanding; like you would any other person without sickle cell disease." Kiera raised her hand and said, "We can help Kayla stay healthy by reminding her to drink water and rest when she needs to." "That's right," said Mr. Whitehurst!

Later, during recess, kids talked to me again and even asked me to play kickball. After the game, Chloe said to me, "I'm really sorry. I didn't know what sickle cell disease was. I just knew you were sick and missed a lot of school. I didn't want that to happen to me." "We're sorry too, Kayla," Amy and Cecelia said. "Will you forgive us? How can we help you stay healthy?" they asked. After exchanging hugs, I spent the rest of recess explaining to my friends how I manage my sickle cell disease and stay healthy.

Kayla's Tips on Managing Sickle Cell Disease

- Good hydration is very important in managing sickle cell disease. Dehydration can cause and/or make a pain crisis worse. Drink at least 64 ounces of water every day to stay well hydrated.

- Eating a well-balanced healthy diet is very important to maintain overall health. Eat plenty of iron-rich foods and stay active to maintain a healthy weight.

- Extreme changes in body temperature could trigger a pain crisis. Try to transition slowly from different environmental temperatures. Dress warmly when it is cold outside. Don't get in a swimming pool where the water is too cold. Take frequent breaks and rest while doing physical activities.

- Regular medical check-ups with your hematologist is crucial. Discuss a pain management plan with your doctor. Make sure your pain medications are secure and you have quick access to them when needed.

- Know your triggers. Infection, fatigue, and dehydration are possible triggers for a pain crisis. Do everything you can to avoid your triggers.

- If you develop a fever of 101.1 degrees Fahrenheit or higher, go to the emergency room right away. Don't wait! You could have an infection that may cause serious complications with your health.

- Take your medicine. Make sure you take your prescription medicine as directed. Get vaccines, medical treatments, and lab tests that your doctor recommends.

- Stress and emotional issues can trigger a pain crisis. Lean on others for support and talk to a therapist if needed.

About the Authors

Jaime Mahaffey, MSW, LISW, is a social worker with several years of experience working with children with chronic medical conditions. She is also the mother of a special little girl who was diagnosed with sickle cell disease shortly after birth. Jaime has a master's degree in Social Work from the University of Cincinnati and is a Licensed Independent Social Worker. She is passionate about connecting with families and providing quality health education in a manner that is relatable and easy to understand.

Jaime has spent the last 14 years learning about sickle cell disease and helping her daughter navigate a world full of fear and lack of understanding about sickle cell disease. Jaime and her daughter hope to be a source of inspiration and support to other families affected by sickle cell disease. It is Jaime's greatest hope that one day there will be a cure for sickle cell disease. But, until then, she wants her daughter and all individuals living with sickle cell disease to know that life is a beautiful gift and there is no limit to what you can achieve.

Kristy High, M.Ed, is a health and wellness educator with several years of experience working with the pediatric population and educating people on various health and wellness topics that are prominent today. Kristy has a master's degree in Health Education, with a concentration in health promotion, from Virginia Tech.

She is passionate about enhancing the knowledge of families and meeting them where they are to assist in improving their quality of life. Her god daughter is her inspiration for writing *I'm No Different Than You*. Her perseverance and positivity has been an inspiration to others living with sickle cell disease. This book is a reminder to her god daughter, and others living with sickle cell disease, that you are not alone and it is possible to live a happy and healthy life!

Made in the USA
Coppell, TX
14 October 2023

22854646R00024